Key Stage Two Maths Investigations

Teacher Book for Year 4

This Teacher Book accompanies CGP's Year 4 Maths Investigations Question Book.

It's matched page-to-page with the Question Book and includes background information to help teachers introduce and teach each investigation. Detailed answers are included too!

We've also made some handy printable resources to go alongside the investigations — you can download them from this page:

www.cgpbooks.co.uk/KS2-Maths-Investigations

Or you can scan this QR code:

What CGP is all about

Our sole aim here at CGP is to produce the highest quality books — carefully written, immaculately presented and dangerously close to being funny.

Then we work our socks off to get them out to you — at the cheapest possible prices.

Contents

Section One — Number, Addition and Subtraction

Section Two — Multiplication and Division

Contents

Published by CGP

ISBN: 978 1 78908 900 4

Written by Amanda MacNaughton and Mike Ollerton.

Editors: Ellen Burton, Sharon Keeley-Holden, Sam Norman
Reviewer: Gareth Mitchell
With thanks to Caley Simpson for the proofreading.

Printed by Elanders Ltd, Newcastle upon Tyne.
Clipart from Corel®
Based on the classic CGP style created by Richard Parsons.

How To Use This Book

This book guides teachers through each of the investigations in the pupil book. Each page in the pupil book has an accompanying page in the teacher book, as shown below:

The pupil page, with the answers written on in red.

Introduction to the investigation, and list of its aims.

List of key vocabulary, and list of required resources (if any).

Green boxes explain extra support that can be given to struggling pupils.

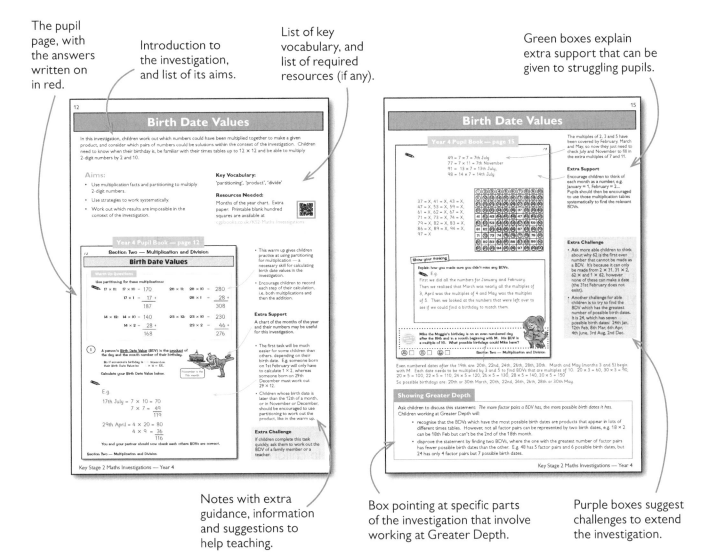

Notes with extra guidance, information and suggestions to help teaching.

Box pointing at specific parts of the investigation that involve working at Greater Depth.

Purple boxes suggest challenges to extend the investigation.

It is a good idea to read through the investigation and teacher notes before delivering each lesson, as this will allow you to prepare, e.g.:

- Required <u>resources</u> – e.g. maths manipulatives or print-outs (some investigations have accompanying printable online resources — these are found at cgpbooks.co.uk/KS2-Maths-Investigations or by scanning the QR code).

- Any other set-up — e.g. some investigations may require children to work in mixed-ability <u>pairings</u> or <u>groups</u>, and some may benefit from a large <u>space</u> being available.

- <u>Timings</u> — investigations could take varying lengths of time, depending on the learners and environment you are working in. You might need to be prepared with the suggested extra challenges, if you expect some children to finish early.

The next page gives more general advice for leading these investigations.

How To Use This Book

During the Lesson

- There will be many opportunities throughout these investigations to stop the lesson for a <u>mini-plenary</u> or quick class discussion.
- Ask the children what they have found out so far or what they have noticed.
- Ask children to demonstrate how they are being <u>systematic</u>.
- Regularly remind children that good mathematicians <u>test ideas</u> and <u>predictions</u>; they get things wrong sometimes and learn from it.
- Ask children at the end of sessions to talk about the maths skills they have used today.

Greater Depth

Each investigation provides opportunities for children to demonstrate '<u>Greater Depth</u>'.
These require not only mastery of the mathematical concept being taught, but also skills such as:

- <u>analysis</u> (breaking down a problem into its component parts).
- <u>synthesis</u> (bringing different mathematical concepts together).
- <u>metacognition</u> (reflecting on what and how they are learning).
- <u>creativity</u> (transferring their understanding to a new situation).

Skills Needed for Completing Investigations

Maths investigations involve a special set of skills that help children to deal with mathematical situations in real life. They need to:

- <u>work systematically</u> (collect and work out information in an orderly way).
- <u>spot patterns</u> and <u>make predictions</u> (use evidence to decide what will happen next).
- <u>generate rules</u> (use evidence to make generalisations).
- <u>show their thinking</u> (write down their thoughts and findings).

Introduce pupils to these skills using pages 1-2 of the workbook.

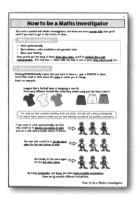

'Showing your thinking' is often called 'Journaling'. It helps children develop their reasoning skills. Thinking more deeply about the maths they are doing will help them to master mathematical concepts and show greater depth in their work.

Talk them through the examples and invite them to think of other examples of where they could apply these skills (e.g. in Science or Computer Science).

Negative Numbers

Children need to know that negative numbers are numbers less than zero: –1, –2, –3, –4, –5, … and also know them as minus numbers. Children will be generating their own calculations from number cards they make. They'll be making predictions, writing down their thinking and trying to be methodical in their recording.

Aims:

- Increase fluency in calculations using negative numbers.

- Look for patterns in order to aid systematic working.

- Understand and use the terms maximum and minimum.

Key Vocabulary:
'maximum', 'minimum', 'minus', 'negative'

Resources Needed:
Paper or card for cards to be made from.

Year 4 Pupil Book — page 3

Section One — Number, Addition and Subtraction   3

Negative Numbers

Warm Up Questions

1) What happens when you take 8 away from 5? Discuss with a partner.

2) What does this calculation look like? Draw your ideas below.

8 7 6 5 4 3 2 1

–3   0   5

① Make five cards — one showing an equals sign, one showing a subtraction sign, and the others showing any three 1-digit numbers.

E.g. if you choose the numbers 3, 1 and 7, you'll have these five cards:

= – 3 1 7

② Use your cards to make some different calculations and work out the answers. You can put two of the digits together to make a 2-digit number. Write down your calculations below.

With the numbers 3, 1 and 7, here are some of the calculations you could make:
7 – 1 = 6
7 – 13 = –6
17 – 3 = 14
3 – 7 = –4

E.g.
13 – 7 = 6
7 – 13 = –6
1 – 3 = –2
1 – 7 = –6
7 – 3 = 4

Section One — Number, Addition and Subtraction

- Discussion could involve the fact this gives an answer below zero/a negative number, and that the answer is –3.

- It is important that children don't simply focus on the answer, but that the answer is negative. They may discuss why, e.g. because 8 has a greater value than 5, so when you subtract it, you have to count below zero.

Extra Support

Encourage children to draw a number line if they don't have their own ideas. The number line could be vertical, like a thermometer.

- Children should find a range of answers that are both negative and positive.

- At this stage, the calculations do not need to be in any particular order or recorded systematically.

- As the aside comment shows, not every digit has to be used in each calculation.

Extra Support

- Children who need additional support could be encouraged to use a number line provided by the teacher, or practise drawing their own number line.

- They could also be encouraged to focus on 1-digit calculations first, before putting digits together.

Negative Numbers

4

(3) What do you think the <u>maximum</u> and <u>minimum</u> possible answers to your calculations will be? Write down the two calculations below.

Maximum: E.g. 73 – 1 = 72

Minimum: E.g. 1 – 73 = –72

Show your thinking

Write a rule about how to find a maximum and a minimum using a set of number cards.

E.g. To find the maximum answer, subtract the smallest digit from the largest 2-digit number you can make.

To find the minimum answer, subtract the largest 2-digit number you can make from the smallest digit.

- Children may notice that to find the minimum answer you swap the numbers around in the calculation for the maximum answer.

- It is important that they know the difference between a digit and a number – this will help make their reasoning clearer.

Make sure your rule is <u>general</u> — it needs to work for all numbers.

Make sure children understand this concept — when they come up with a rule, it should be <u>general</u>, meaning it always works, rather than being specific to certain circumstances.

Section One — Number, Addition and Subtraction

Negative Numbers

Year 4 Pupil Book — page 5

5

(4) Now it's time to find **all** the possible calculations you can make with your cards. Write down your calculations below.

> Think about the order in which you are going to work — this will help you to work systematically. Discuss your approach with a partner.

E.g.

$1 - 73 = -72$
$1 - 37 = -36$
$1 - 7 = -6$
$1 - 3 = -2$

$3 - 71 = -68$
$3 - 17 = -14$
$3 - 7 = -4$
$3 - 1 = 2$

$7 - 31 = -24$
$7 - 13 = -6$
$7 - 3 = 4$
$7 - 1 = 6$

$13 - 7 = 6$

$17 - 3 = 14$

$31 - 7 = 24$

$37 - 1 = 36$

$71 - 3 = 68$

$73 - 1 = 72$

My total number of calculations is: 18

Now Try This: If you add 1 to each of your chosen numbers, will your maximum and minimum answers become higher or lower? Discuss with a partner, then try it out to see if you were right.

Section One — Number, Addition and Subtraction

Working systematically means showing order to their thinking. Children may:

- Begin each calculation with the smallest number possible and increase it when all possibilities are recorded.
- Begin with 1-digit numbers subtracting 2-digit numbers and then 2-digit numbers subtracting 1-digit numbers.
- Begin with the largest number possible and then swap the numbers in the calculation.

Encourage them to look for patterns in their workings e.g.

- When they swap the numbers in the calculation, the answer is the same but swaps from positive to negative, or vice versa:
$73 - 1 = 72$; $1 - 73 = -72$
$7 - 13 = -6$; $13 - 7 = 6$
$17 - 3 = 14$; $3 - 17 = -14$
This means that they should have an even number of calculations — this is one way of checking no answers are missing.
- Noticing the use of odd and even numbers in calculations and whether that produces odd or even numbers in answers.
- When the first number of the calculation is smaller than the second the answer is negative; when the first number is larger than the second, the answer is positive.

Patterns that children have noticed could be shared in a mini-plenary during this activity.

E.g. **=**, **–**, **4**, **2**, **8**

Pupils may talk about the first and second numbers of the calculation being higher than before, making the answer higher than before:
Largest 2-digit number: 84. $84 - 2 = 82$ (higher by 10)

Or, in the case of the negative answer, lower than before:
Smallest single digit: 2. $2 - 84 = -82$ (lower by 10)

They should notice that the maximum and minimum numbers are made up of the same digits and may explain this as being the same amount away from zero.

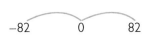

Extra Challenge

Some children may want to take this further and increase the numbers by 1 again to see if they get the same results, i.e. to look for a pattern.

Showing Greater Depth

Children working at Greater Depth will:

- (Q3) come up with a generalisation about how to find the maximum and minimum, based on evidence.

Roman Numerals

In this investigation, children will combine 2 or 3 Roman numerals to generate different numbers. They'll order them on a number line and calculate the differences between them. Before starting the investigation, children should be familiar with Roman numerals and be able to read them to 100 (C).

Aims:

- To write Roman numerals to 100.

- To understand the Roman numeral system, e.g. when I is before X it makes 9 but when I is after X, it makes 11.

- Use logical reasoning to rearrange numerals to create other numbers.

Key Vocabulary:

'Roman numerals', 'minimum', 'maximum'

Resources Needed:

Paper or card for cards to be made from

Year 4 Pupil Book — page 6

6

Roman Numerals

Warm Up Questions

1) Using Roman numerals, complete the missing numbers on the clock.

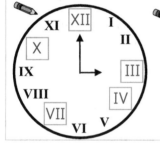

2) Complete the chart below.

Roman Numeral	Value	Number
XIII	10 + 1 + 1 + 1	13
XXV	10 + 10 + 5	25
XL	50 – 10	40
XC	100 – 10	90

I = 1
V = 5
X = 10
L = 50
C = 100

(1) A Roman numeral can be a number <u>on its own</u>, or can be combined with other numerals to make <u>different numbers</u>. Complete the table showing the <u>different numbers</u> that can be made with <u>different pairs</u>. Each number can use one or both of the numerals. Only use each numeral <u>once</u> in a number.

[I] and [V]	[I] and [X]	[V] and [X]
I , IV, V, VI	I, IX, X, XI	V, X, XV

With I and V, <u>four different numbers</u> can be made. Can you make the same number of different numbers with the other pairs? Why is this?

I & V and I & X make 4 different numbers, whereas V & X only make 3 different numbers.

This is because I can be placed before V and X, but V cannot be placed before X.

Section One — Number, Addition and Subtraction

- This warm up should remind children of the importance of placing Roman numerals correctly. For example, 9 is shown by placing I in front of X, and 90 is shown by placing X in front of C. 4 is shown by placing I in front of V, and 40 is shown by placing X in front of L.

- The 'value' column breaks the number down into each Roman numeral, so 25 is not 20 + 5 but 10 + 10 + 5, as there is no single Roman numeral for 20.

- It may be interesting to discuss with the children how the maximum values are created by these pairs of Roman numerals.

- Children might notice that the maximum value is created by the larger numeral followed by the smaller numeral.

Extra Support

If children struggle to notice this relationship, try writing the different combinations for each pair one above the other, i.e.:

I	IV	V	VI
I	IX	X	XI
V		X	XV

This will make it easier for children to see which is missing from the final set.

Roman Numerals

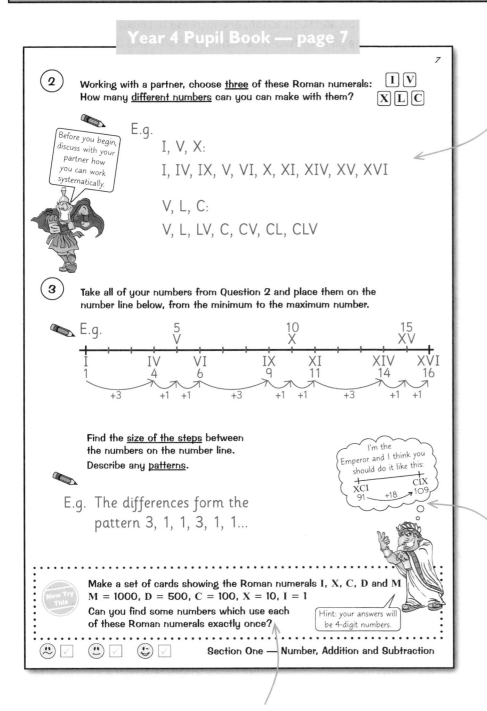

- Encourage children to work systematically so they don't miss any possibilities. For example, they could begin with the smallest numeral, then place increasingly larger numerals next to it.

- There are 15 possible arrangements of three Roman numerals, e.g. for I, V, X:
I, V, X
IV, IX, VI, VX, XI, XV
IVX, IXV, VIX, VXI, XIV, XVI.
However, these aren't all numbers in the Roman numeral system, e.g. VX isn't valid (this would be 5, which of course is represented by just V).

- Some non-genuine numbers are trickier to spot, e.g. VL looks like it might be 45, but 45 is instead represented by XLV. To make it easier to check combinations, there are lots of lists of Roman numerals on the internet.

Time could be given at the end of the lesson for pupils to discuss the numbers they chose and outline any patterns they discovered. Patterns in the differences will vary depending on the three Roman numerals used (and there may not always be a pattern).
For V, L, C, the numbers in order are: 5, 50, 55, 100, 105, 150, 155. The pattern in the differences is: 5, 45, 5, 45...

MDCXI = 1611   MDCIX = 1609   MDXCI = 1591   MCDXI = 1411   MCDIX = 1409

To include all five of the Roman numerals, each number must start with M, which will then be followed by either D or CD. There are only five possibilities, but it is expected that children will experiment with many different orders of the numerals before establishing which are genuine numbers.

Showing Greater Depth

Children working at Greater Depth will:

- (Q2) devise a system to generate all possible combinations of the set of three numerals.
- (Now Try This) devise strategies to eliminate groups of permutations of Roman numerals (e.g. realising that combinations that start with I, X or C cannot be genuine numbers and can safely be ignored).

Addition and Subtraction Puzzles

In this investigation, children will develop fluency in addition and subtraction, and increase familiarity with the 11 and 9 times tables. It involves children making pairs of two-digit numbers which have the same digits but in the opposite order. They then add the pairs and search for patterns in the totals. The investigation is then repeated using subtraction.

Aims:

- Add and subtract 2-digit numbers efficiently, using any method.
- Recognise patterns in groups of numbers.
- Use what they notice to draw conclusions.

Key Vocabulary:

'consecutive'

Resources Needed:

None

Year 4 Pupil Book — page 8

8

Addition and Subtraction Puzzles

Warm Up Questions

Complete these additions:

30 + 80 = 110	4 + 9 = 13	40 + 60 + 5 + 7 = 112
40 + 70 = 110	17 + 7 = 24	70 + 50 + 4 + 9 = 133
50 + 90 = 140	15 + 8 = 23	80 + 40 + 3 + 8 = 131

(1)
- Write down any **2-digit number**.
- **Reverse** the digits to produce a second number.
- **Add** the two numbers.

E.g. 83 + 38 = 121   or   21 + 12 = 33

Add the numbers using any method you like.

Create at least 8 additions. Record them below.

E.g.
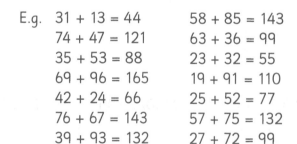

31 + 13 = 44	58 + 85 = 143
74 + 47 = 121	63 + 36 = 99
35 + 53 = 88	23 + 32 = 55
69 + 96 = 165	19 + 91 = 110
42 + 24 = 66	25 + 52 = 77
76 + 67 = 143	57 + 75 = 132
39 + 93 = 132	27 + 72 = 99

Section One — Number, Addition and Subtraction

This warm up involves adding multiples of 10 and adding on single-digit numbers. It will prepare children for the first part of the investigation.

If available, 9-sided dice can be used to generate the digits.

- If time is limited, pairs of children could combine their sums to produce a larger set of examples which will show the pattern more clearly.

- Watch out for repeated calculations in a different order, e.g. 31 + 13 then 13 + 31.

Addition and Subtraction Puzzles

Extra Support

Prompt children with questions if they struggle to notice the patterns:

- Are any of your answers the same?

- What do you notice about the 2-digit answers?

- Look at the last digits of the 3-digit answers — what do you notice?

- Does your partner have any answers that are the same?

- Do any of the answers appear in the same times table?

The final question will only be relevant to children who are familiar with the 11 times tables (which may depend on what time of year this investigation is completed).

Setting the sum out in columns can help make this clearer.

- To understand why the patterns exist, children should look for relationships between the pairs of numbers and their sums.

- They should be encouraged to show their understanding with examples.

9

② **What do you notice about your answers?**

Look at your partner's answers too and see if they show the same thing.

- Some of the answers are the same, e.g. 99, 143.
- 2-digit answers have repeated digits, e.g. 66, 77.
- The answers are all multiples of 11.
- In the 3-digit answers, the middle digit is always 1 more than the last digit.

Show your thinking

Why do you think your sums show these patterns?

Use examples to help explain your ideas.

To get 2-digit answers, you add the same digits for the tens as for the ones. This means the digits of the answer are the same. E.g. 35 + 53: in the tens place there is 3 + 5, and in the ones place there is 5 + 3. These both make 8, so the sum is 88.

Some answers are the same because different pairs of digits add to the same number, e.g. 5 + 4, 3 + 6 and 2 + 7 all make 9.

With 3-digit answers, the ones in the sum add up to at least 10, meaning there's an extra 10 in the tens place.

Section One — Number, Addition and Subtraction

Whilst some children might notice the middle digit of 3-digit answers is one more than the final digit, it is quite tricky to explain why this is.
Setting several of the calculations out as shown below can help children understand and put into words the reason for the pattern:
E.g. 38 + 83:   30 + 80 = 110
                           8 + 3 = 11
                                         121

Addition and Subtraction Puzzles

10

3 Now you're going to repeat the investigation using subtraction.
- Write down any <u>2-digit number</u>.
- <u>Reverse</u> the digits to produce a second number.
- Find the <u>difference</u> between the two numbers.

> Subtract the smaller number from the bigger number using any method you like.

E.g. $83 - 38 = \underline{45}$ or $21 - 12 = \underline{9}$

Find at least 8 different subtractions. Record them below.

 E.g.

$43 - 34 = 9$	$93 - 39 = 54$
$74 - 47 = 27$	$85 - 58 = 27$
$53 - 35 = 18$	$63 - 36 = 27$
$96 - 69 = 27$	$75 - 57 = 18$
$42 - 24 = 18$	$91 - 19 = 72$
$87 - 78 = 9$	$73 - 37 = 36$

4 What do you notice about your answers?

> Remember to include some examples.

- Some of the answers are the same, e.g. 18, 27.
- All of the answers, except for 9, have 2 digits.
- The answers are all multiples of 9.
- The digits in the answers add to make 9,
  e.g. in 63, 6 + 3 = 9.

> Look at your partner's answers too and see if they show the same thing.

Section One — Number, Addition and Subtraction

- The larger the pool of numbers pupils have, the more likely they are to spot a pattern. They could combine their examples with a partner's to produce a larger pool of examples.

- In each subtraction, the number in the ones place is greater in the number being subtracted than it is in the larger number. This may mean that counting up or subtracting a near multiple of ten then adjusting are more efficient methods to use than partitioning or column subtraction.

Extra Support

Prompt children with questions if they struggle to notice the patterns:

- How many digits do the answers have?

- Write the answers out in order. What do you notice about the digits in the answers?

- Are any of the answers the same as each other?

- Do any of the answers appear in the same times table?

Children should be familiar with the patterns in the 9 times table so should see the connection between the two digits of the answers.

Addition and Subtraction Puzzles

11

Show your thinking

Why do you think your answers are like this?

 E.g.

Some answers are the same because the difference between the tens digits in both questions is the same, as is the difference between the ones digits, e.g. 42 – 24 and 53 – 35.

The digits in the answer add to make 9 because they're all multiples of 9, and the digits of multiples of 9 add up to 9.

Extra Support

- Encourage children who are unsure how to begin to think about the ones digits first, as these must add to give a number ending in 3. Therefore the ones could be 6 and 7, 5 and 8, or 4 and 9.

- From this they can generate their 2-digit numbers: 67 + 76, 58 + 85, 49 + 94. (They may already have found these in Question 1.)

- They should then try the subtractions (or look back at their answers to Question 3) to work out which pair gives the answer 27.

(5) Two 2-digit numbers, where one has the other's digits reversed, have a total of 143 and a difference of 27. What could those two numbers be?

58 and 85

58 + 85 = 143
85 – 58 = 27

1) Choose two consecutive 1-digit numbers, e.g. 4 and 5.
2) Use them to make two 3-digit numbers that are the same forwards and backwards, e.g. 454 and 545.
3) Subtract one number from the other, e.g. 545 – 454 = 91.
4) Repeat steps 1-3 with lots of pairs of consecutive 1-digit numbers.

> Consecutive numbers come one after the other.

What do you notice? Can you explain this?

 ☐ ☐ ☐ Section One — Number, Addition and Subtraction

Children will need to try out several subtractions to look for a pattern.

E.g. 212 – 121 = 91
323 – 232 = 91
767 – 676 = 91
878 – 787 = 91

The answer is always 91. This is because the ones value is always 1 more in the larger number than in the smaller number. The tens value is always 1 more in the smaller number than in the larger number.

Extra Challenge

Pupils could undertake a similar activity that involves addition instead of subtraction, then have a go at describing what they notice and suggesting why.

Showing Greater Depth

Children working at Greater Depth will:

- (Q2) be able to use ideas of place value and carrying to explain why, when two pairs of 'reversed digit' numbers are added to produce a 3-digit number, the middle digit is always one more than the last digit.

- (Now Try This) be able to explain the result using the idea that a greater number of tens in the number being subtracted makes the exchange of a hundred for 10 tens necessary.

Birth Date Values

In this investigation, children work out which numbers could have been multiplied together to make a given product, and consider which pairs of numbers could be solutions within the context of the investigation. Children need to know when their birthday is, be familiar with their times tables up to 12 × 12 and be able to multiply 2-digit numbers by 2 and 10.

Aims:

- Use multiplication facts and partitioning to multiply 2-digit numbers.
- Use strategies to work systematically.
- Work out which results are impossible in the context of the investigation.

Key Vocabulary:

'partitioning', 'product', 'divide'

Resources Needed:

Months of the year chart. Extra paper. Printable blank hundred squares are available at cgpbooks.co.uk/KS2-Maths-Investigations

---

Year 4 Pupil Book — page 12

12   **Section Two — Multiplication and Division**

Birth Date Values

Warm Up Questions

Use partitioning for these multiplications:

17 × 11: 17 × 10 = 170   28 × 11: 28 × 10 = 280
         17 × 1 = 17 +   28 × 1 = 28 +
                  187   308

14 × 12: 14 × 10 = 140   23 × 12: 23 × 10 = 230
         14 × 2 = 28 +   23 × 2 = 46 +
                  168   276

(1) A person's **Birth Date Value** (BDV) is the **product** of the day and the month number of their birthday.

So if someone's birthday is 5th November, their Birth Date Value is: 5 × 11 = 55.

Calculate your Birth Date Value below.

November is the 11th month.

E.g.

17th July = 7 × 10 = 70
            7 × 7 = 49
                    119

29th April = 4 × 20 = 80
             4 × 9 = 36
                     116

You and your partner should now check each others BDVs are correct.

Section Two — Multiplication and Division

- This warm up gives children practice at using partitioning for multiplication — a necessary skill for calculating birth date values in the investigation.

- Encourage children to record each step of their calculation, i.e. both multiplications and then the addition.

Extra Support

A chart of the months of the year and their numbers may be useful for this investigation.

- The first task will be much easier for some children than others, depending on their birth date. E.g. someone born on 1st February will only have to calculate 1 × 2, whereas someone born on 29th December must work out 29 × 12.

- Children whose birth date is later than the 12th of a month, or in November or December, should be encouraged to use partitioning to work out the product, like in the warm up.

Extra Challenge

If children complete this task quickly, ask them to work out the BDV of a family member or a teacher.

Birth Date Values

- You'll almost certainly have to direct children to order themselves to avoid total chaos. Depending on the ability of the class, this activity can either be done as a whole class or in smaller groups of e.g. 10.

- However, the greater the number of children involved, the greater the chance of a shared BDV, which is useful for the next few questions.

Year 4 Pupil Book — page 13

13

(2) Write your BDV on a blank piece of paper. You and your classmates should now arrange yourselves in order of BDV (from smallest to biggest). Record all the BDVs in order below.

E.g.
Sara: 4   Holly: 60   Forrest: 116
Luke: 17   Tomasz: 60   Max: 208
Hiram: 44   Aaliyah: 80   Hannah: 210
Aki: 48   Lin: 88   Mira: 270

Show your thinking

If two people have the same BDV, they must have the same birthday. Is this true or false? Explain your answer.

 E.g.

It is false. The day and month number could just multiply to give the same product. E.g. Holly and Tomasz have the same BDV, but Holly's birthday is 6th October and Tomasz's is 12th May.
6 × 10 and 12 × 5 are both 60.

Section Two — Multiplication and Division

- If space is limited, you could simply place the pieces of paper (with names added) in a line, or perhaps go into the hall/playground.

- Encourage discussion between the children about who should stand where so there is enough space for everyone.

- Ask the children to decide what they should do when more than one pupil has the same BDV. E.g. they might decide they should stand next to each other, or behind each other.

- When they are stood in order, ask why they think some people have the same BDV. Ask children with the same BDV when their birthdays are. They may share a birthday, or have different birth dates which create the same product using different numbers.

Extra Challenge

Interestingly, two children in the class having the same birthday is more likely than you'd expect. In a group of 23, there's roughly a 50% chance of two people sharing a birthday.

Children could test this idea using a random number generator with a maximum number of 365. How many numbers do they need to generate before getting a repeat?

Birth Date Values

14

(3) Ciara's BDV is 44. What could her birthday be?

4th November (4 × 11) or 11th April (11 × 4)
or 22nd February (22 × 2)

(4) Choose someone in the class whose birthday you don't know. Use their BDV to work out when their birthday could be.

There could be more than one possible birthday.

E.g. Lin: 88
22 × 4 = 88, 8 × 11 = 88,
11 × 8 = 88
So 22nd April, 8th November
and 11th August are possible.

30 days has September,
April, June and November
All the rest have 31, except
for February with 28 clear
And 29 in each leap year.

Then <u>check</u> with the person whose BDV you chose. Was it one of the options you worked out? Yes, Lin's birthday is 11th August.

(5) With a partner, work out <u>which numbers</u> between 1 and 100 can be a BDV. Circle numbers that can be BDVs on the hundred square on the next page.

Think about how you can work systematically to make sure you don't miss any numbers.

1st to 31st January = 1 to 31
1st to 29th February
= all the even numbers up to 58.
1st to 31st March
= all the multiples of 3 up to 93.
April = all multiples of 4
May = all multiples of 5

Section Two — Multiplication and Division

Extra Support

For children who are struggling, ask them what two numbers multiply together to make 44. This is likely to generate the numbers 4 and 11. Eliciting from pupils that 44 is even should guide them to spotting that we can multiply something by 2 to get 44.

- Children should recognise that two numbers that multiply to make the product or BDV can create two different birthdays but only if both of the numbers are between 1 and 12.

- That's why there are three possible birthdays here. Two come from 8 × 11, but only one comes from 22 × 4, because there isn't a 22nd month in the year.

- Starting with January means the numbers 1-31 can be circled straight away.

- Children may need extra paper to systematically check each day of the year. However, they will find it quicker either checking each number on the 100 square from 32 onwards, or using patterns, as in the example answer.

Children need to know how many days each month has (the rhyme on this page will help).

Birth Date Values

15

49 = 7 × 7 = 7th July
77 = 7 × 11 = 7th November
91 = 13 × 7 = 13th July,
98 = 14 × 7 = 14th July

Check any numbers that haven't been crossed out to make sure they aren't possible BDVs:

37 = X, 41 = X, 43 = X,
47 = X, 53 = X, 59 = X,
61 = X, 62 = X, 67 = X,
71 = X, 73 = X, 74 = X,
79 = X, 82 = X, 83 = X,
86 = X, 89 = X, 94 = X,
97 = X

①	②	③	④	⑤	⑥	⑦	⑧	⑨	⑩
⑪	⑫	⑬	⑭	⑮	⑯	⑰	⑱	⑲	⑳
㉑	㉒	㉓	㉔	㉕	㉖	㉗	㉘	㉙	㉚
㉛	㉜	㉝	㉞	㉟	㊱	37	㊳	㊴	㊵
41	㊷	43	㊹	㊺	㊻	47	㊽	㊾	㊿
51	52	53	54	55	56	57	58	59	60
61	62	63	64	65	66	67	68	69	70
71	72	73	74	75	76	77	78	79	80
81	82	83	84	85	86	87	88	89	90
91	92	93	94	95	96	97	98	99	100

Show your thinking

Explain how you made sure you didn't miss any BDVs.

E.g.

First we did all the numbers for January and February. Then we realised that March was nearly all the multiples of 3, April was the multiples of 4 and May was the multiples of 5. Then we looked at the numbers that were left over to see if we could find a birthday to match them.

Now Try This

Mike the Moggie's birthday is on an even-numbered day after the 19th and in a month beginning with M. His BDV is a multiple of 10. What possible birthdays could Mike have?

Section Two — Multiplication and Division

The multiples of 2, 3 and 5 have been covered by February, March and May, so now they just need to check July and November to fill in the extra multiples of 7 and 11.

Extra Support

Encourage children to think of each month as a number, e.g. January = 1, February = 2... Pupils should then be encouraged to use those multiplication tables systematically to find the relevant BDVs.

Extra Challenge

- Ask more able children to think about why 62 is the first even number that cannot be made as a BDV. It's because it can only be made from 2 × 31, 31 × 2, 62 × 1 and 1 × 62, however none of these can make a date (the 31st February does not exist).

- Another challenge for able children is to try to find the BDV which has the greatest number of possible birth dates. It is 24, which has seven possible birth dates: 24th Jan, 12th Feb, 8th Mar, 6th Apr, 4th June, 3rd Aug, 2nd Dec.

Even-numbered dates after the 19th are: 20th, 22nd, 24th, 26th, 28th, 30th. March and May (months 3 and 5) begin with M. Each date needs to be multiplied by 3 and 5 to find BDVs that are multiples of 10: 20 × 3 = 60, 30 × 3 = 90, 20 × 5 = 100, 22 × 5 = 110, 24 × 5 = 120, 26 × 5 = 130, 28 × 5 = 140, 30 × 5 = 150

So possible birthdays are: 20th or 30th March, 20th, 22nd, 24th, 26th, 28th or 30th May.

Showing Greater Depth

Ask children to discuss this statement: *The more factor pairs a BDV has, the more possible birth dates it has.* Children working at Greater Depth will:

- recognise that the BDVs which have the most possible birth dates are products that appear in lots of different times tables. However, not all factor pairs can be represented by two birth dates, e.g. 18 × 2 can be 18th Feb but can't be the 2nd of the 18th month.

- disprove the statement by finding two BDVs, where the one with the greater number of factor pairs has fewer possible birth dates than the other. E.g. 48 has 5 factor pairs and 6 possible birth dates, but 24 has only 4 factor pairs but 7 possible birth dates.

Factor Pairs

The first part of the investigation involves children physically arranging themselves into groups. They will then link grouping to factors, and investigate how many factors different numbers have. Children need to be familiar with their times tables up to 12 × 12, but don't have to know them by heart. For the first two tasks, small mixed-ability groups can be chosen, then the third task will involve most of the class.

Aims:

- Use multiplication facts.

- Use visual aids to help understanding of factors.

- Understand and use the terms groupings and factors.

- Show some order to their working.

Key Vocabulary:

'factors'

Resources Needed:

Space for pupils to stand in groups

Year 4 Pupil Book — page 16

16

Factor Pairs

Warm Up Questions

Draw a line from each circled number to the correct multiplications.

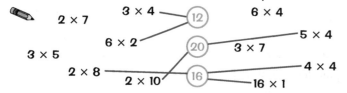

Once the warm up activity has been completed, ask the children what it shows them about the numbers 12, 20 and 16.
They should recognise that these numbers appear in different times tables and can be made by multiplying more than one pair of numbers.

(1) Your teacher will choose <u>six children</u> to stand at the front of the class. They have to split themselves into <u>equal-sized groups</u> in as many ways as they can. Draw how they split themselves up below. There are four possible ways.

Start off with 1 group of 6...

- Children can choose how they record the groupings. For example, they might draw dots or dashes rather than stick-people, or write a description in words.

- It is important to emphasise that 2 groups of 3 and 3 groups of 2 are two different ways of splitting up the group. This is a useful demonstration of commutativity.

What do you notice about these groups? Think about what you know about factor pairs.

What if it was a group of 8? Well, the number of different <u>groupings</u> for 8 is the same as the number of <u>factors</u> of 8:

There are 4 different groupings for 8: 1 group of ⑧, 2 groups of ④, 4 groups of ② and 8 groups of ①.

So there are 4 factors of 8: 1, 2, 4 and 8.

Section Two — Multiplication and Division

Factor Pairs

17

2 Your teacher will now choose <u>five children</u> to do the same.
Draw the ways that they split themselves up below.

There are __2__ different groupings so there are __2__ factors of 5.
The factors of 5 are: ___1 and 5___ .

> Children might think that the reason why a group of 5 cannot be grouped in any other ways is because 5 is an odd number. This misconception will be challenged in a later example.

3 Now <u>24 children</u> (yes, 24!) will now split themselves into <u>equal-sized</u> groups in as many different ways as they can. Record the different groupings below.

> The remaining children in the class can be directors — make sure every possibly answer is found and that all answers are recorded.

There are __8__ different groupings so there are __8__ factors of 24.
The factors of 24 are: __1, 2, 3, 4, 6, 8, 12 and 24__ .

Section Two — Multiplication and Division

- Encourage children to work systematically by asking them what the biggest or smallest group size they can make is. Then decrease or increase the group size gradually.

- Children should be beginning to recognise the link between the number of groups, the size of the groups and times tables, e.g. 3 groups of 8 children = 3 × 8 = 24.

- In smaller schools, a smaller number can be used. If a group of 18 is used, there would be 6 different groupings, and therefore 6 factors: 1, 2, 3, 6, 9, and 18. Alternatively, pegs or counters could be used instead of children.

Extra Challenge

With this example, they're likely to see that the factors form pairs — e.g. 2 and 12 are a factor pair of 24. As an extension task, higher ability pupils can discuss this with a teacher, e.g. the idea that there can be 2 groups of 12 or 12 groups of 2.

Factor Pairs

18

(4) How many different groupings would there be with <u>9 children</u>?

There are ..3.. different groupings so there are ..3.. factors of 9.
The factors of 9 are: .....1, 3 and 9.......... .

Show your thinking

9 has an <u>odd</u> number of factors. Why do you think this is?

3 groups of 3 children is 3 × 3.
This can only be written in one way as
the numbers being multiplied are the
same. All the other factors are in pairs.

5, 6 and 24 all had an even number of factors.

(5) Find some other numbers which have an <u>odd number</u> of factors.

2 × 2 = 4   The factors of 4 are 1, 2 and 4.

4 × 4 = 16   The factors of 16 are 1, 2, 4, 8 and 16.

5 × 5 = 25   The factors of 25 are 1, 5 and 25.

So 4, 16 and 25 also have an odd number of factors.

Section Two — Multiplication and Division

- This challenges the common misconception that 5 has only 2 different groupings (factors) because it is an odd number. 9 is an odd number but has more than 2 factors.

- It is of course the prime numbers that have 2 different groupings, because a prime number has exactly 2 factors, 1 and itself. Children will meet prime numbers (and prime factors) in Year 5.

Extra Challenge

This activity could be extended by asking pupils to find odd numbers other than 9 that have more than 2 factors. 15 is the only other odd number less than 20 to have more than 2 factors (1, 3, 5, 15). Beyond that, pupils might find 21, 25, 27 etc.

- Children are not expected to know the term 'square number' until Year 5.

- They should instead recognise that numbers have factor pairs and sometimes one of those pairs is made up of the same number, so cannot be reversed.

- Children may start systematically finding the factors of numbers starting with 1, 2, 3, 4…
  Although this is usually a good approach, after the number 4 it will take quite a while to find the next number with an odd number of factors (9, which has already been found, and then 16).

- Instead, encourage them to look at what made 9 have an odd number of factors (3 × 3).
  Ask them to calculate 2 x 2. Does this give them another number with an odd number of factors?

Factor Pairs

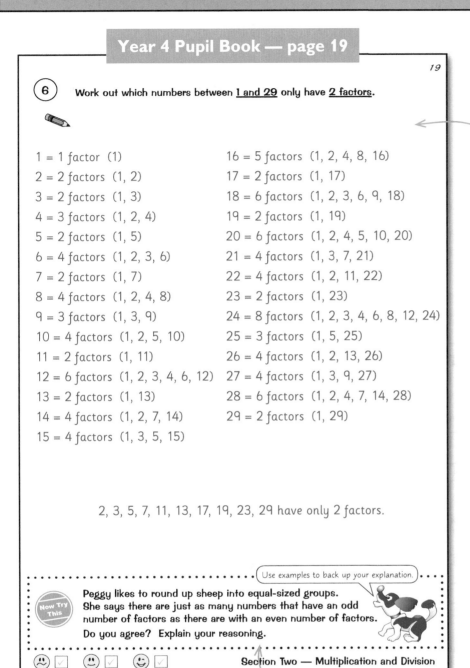

Year 4 Pupil Book — page 19

19

(6) Work out which numbers between <u>1 and 29</u> only have <u>2 factors</u>.

1 = 1 factor (1)
2 = 2 factors (1, 2)
3 = 2 factors (1, 3)
4 = 3 factors (1, 2, 4)
5 = 2 factors (1, 5)
6 = 4 factors (1, 2, 3, 6)
7 = 2 factors (1, 7)
8 = 4 factors (1, 2, 4, 8)
9 = 3 factors (1, 3, 9)
10 = 4 factors (1, 2, 5, 10)
11 = 2 factors (1, 11)
12 = 6 factors (1, 2, 3, 4, 6, 12)
13 = 2 factors (1, 13)
14 = 4 factors (1, 2, 7, 14)
15 = 4 factors (1, 3, 5, 15)

16 = 5 factors (1, 2, 4, 8, 16)
17 = 2 factors (1, 17)
18 = 6 factors (1, 2, 3, 6, 9, 18)
19 = 2 factors (1, 19)
20 = 6 factors (1, 2, 4, 5, 10, 20)
21 = 4 factors (1, 3, 7, 21)
22 = 4 factors (1, 2, 11, 22)
23 = 2 factors (1, 23)
24 = 8 factors (1, 2, 3, 4, 6, 8, 12, 24)
25 = 3 factors (1, 5, 25)
26 = 4 factors (1, 2, 13, 26)
27 = 4 factors (1, 3, 9, 27)
28 = 6 factors (1, 2, 4, 7, 14, 28)
29 = 2 factors (1, 29)

2, 3, 5, 7, 11, 13, 17, 19, 23, 29 have only 2 factors.

Use examples to back up your explanation.

Now Try This

Peggy likes to round up sheep into equal-sized groups.
She says there are just as many numbers that have an odd
number of factors as there are with an even number of factors.
Do you agree? Explain your reasoning.

☺ ☑   ☺ ☑   ☺ ☑

Section Two — Multiplication and Division

- For this question, children should be encouraged to work systematically by finding factor pairs of numbers starting from 1. If a number has a factor pair other than 1 and itself, they can eliminate it. Some numbers were looked at earlier in the investigation (e.g. 6, 9, 24) so can be eliminated straight away.

- After this task, have a discussion with the class about how, when a number only has two factors, they are always 1 and the number itself.

Extra Support

If there isn't a large amount of time left, or if pupils are struggling, they could be encouraged to work in pairs or groups, with pupils taking a series of numbers each and working out how many factors each has. E.g. one pupil takes numbers 1-5, another takes numbers 6-10, etc.

E.g. I do not agree. For the numbers 1 to 29, only 5 numbers have an odd number of factors, but 24 numbers have an even number of factors. Only numbers that are products of a number multiplied by itself have an odd number of factors, and there are far fewer of these than other numbers.

Showing Greater Depth

While children are working on Q6, ask them whether they need to work out every single factor of a number to be able to say how many factors it has. Children working at Greater Depth will recognise that:

- Each factor in the second half of the factor set matches up with a factor in the first half of the set. This means that when you get to a factor which forms a pair with one you have already listed, you can stop and just double the factors written so far (not including the paired factor).

- This doesn't work with square numbers, as the middle factor is multiplied by itself, so you must double the factors in the first half and subtract 1. (Note that pupils do not need to know the term 'square number' yet.)

Partitions and Products

In this investigation, children will be partitioning numbers in various ways and then multiplying those numbers to find different products. Children need to be familiar with their times tables up to 12 × 12, be able to multiply 2-digit numbers by 1-digit numbers and multiply 3 or more 1-digit numbers. They will use their trials with small numbers to identify strategies for partitioning larger numbers in such a way that the largest possible product is generated.

Aims:

- Use multiplication facts, multiply a 2-digit number by a 1-digit number, and multiply three 1-digit numbers.

- Understand and apply the commutative law.

- Look for and use strategies for partitioning numbers in the way that will produce the highest product.

Key Vocabulary:

'partitioning', 'product'

Resources Needed:

Calculators.

Extra Support

If children struggle multiplying three or four numbers, remind them that, because of the commutative law, the order they multiply the numbers in doesn't matter. E.g. instead of doing 7 × 3 × 2 = 21 × 2 = 42 they could do 3 × 2 × 7 = 6 × 7 = 42. This means they are only using times table facts to find the product.

Point out to the children that they need to partition 10 differently in each case. They shouldn't just arrange the same parts in a different order. E.g. 3 + 4 + 3 is the same as 4 + 3 + 3.

As children try to find higher products, ask them if they notice any links between the partitioned sets of numbers and the sizes of the products. They may notice that:

- Multiplying by 1 doesn't make the product any higher, so having lots of 1s in a set produces a low product, e.g. 1 × 1 × 1 × 1 × 1 × 5 = 5.

- Multiplying more numbers together doesn't guarantee a larger product.

Task 3 could be turned into a game for pairs to see who can find the highest possible product, the highest possible product using the fewest numbers, the lowest product using the most numbers, etc.

Year 4 Pupil Book — page 20

20

Partitions and Products

Warm Up Question

Match each multiplication with a product below.

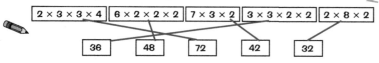

| 2 × 3 × 3 × 4 | 6 × 2 × 2 × 2 | 7 × 3 × 2 | 3 × 3 × 2 × 2 | 2 × 8 × 2 |

| 36 | 48 | 72 | 42 | 32 |

(1) Three different ways of <u>partitioning</u> the number 10 into <u>at least 3 numbers</u> are shown below. Find three more to complete the diagram.

E.g.

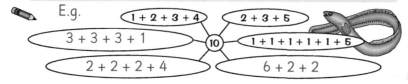

(1 + 2 + 3 + 4) (2 + 3 + 5)

3 + 3 + 3 + 1   10   1 + 1 + 1 + 1 + 1 + 5

2 + 2 + 2 + 4   6 + 2 + 2

(2) Now, turn the addition signs into <u>multiplication signs</u> and find the <u>products</u>.

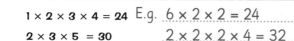

1 × 2 × 3 × 4 = 24   E.g. 6 × 2 × 2 = 24

2 × 3 × 5 = 30   2 × 2 × 2 × 4 = 32

1 × 1 × 1 × 1 × 5 = 5   3 × 3 × 3 × 1 = 27

(3) What was the <u>highest product</u> you found? Can you find a <u>higher product</u> by partitioning 10 in a different way?

E.g. 32 is the highest product made from the lists of partitioned numbers above. A possible higher product is 36 (3 × 3 × 4 or 3 × 3 × 2 × 2).

Section Two — Multiplication and Division

Partitions and Products

There are many ways of partitioning 12. However, now children know that they're going to be trying to find the highest product, they're likely to begin using strategies. Pupils could be encouraged not to use 1, and asked to explain how avoiding 1 is a helpful strategy.

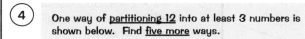

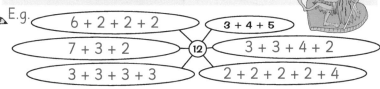

21

4 One way of <u>partitioning 12</u> into at least 3 numbers is shown below. Find <u>five more</u> ways.

E.g.

6 + 2 + 2 + 2   3 + 4 + 5

7 + 3 + 2   **12**   3 + 3 + 4 + 2

3 + 3 + 3 + 3   2 + 2 + 2 + 2 + 4

5 Change the addition signs to <u>multiplication signs</u> and find the <u>products</u>.

E.g. 6 × 2 × 2 × 2 = 48   3 × 4 × 5 = 60
7 × 3 × 2 = 42   3 × 3 × 4 × 2 = 72
3 × 3 × 3 × 3 = 81   2 × 2 × 2 × 2 × 4 = 64

6 What was the <u>highest product</u> you found?
Can you find a <u>higher product</u> by partitioning 12 in a different way?

E.g. 81 was the highest product found.
4 × 4 × 4 = 64
3 × 3 × 6 = 54
I can't find a product higher than 81.

Back your answer up with an example or two.

Show your thinking

Try coming up with a <u>rule</u> for how to partition a number in such a way that multiplying the numbers together would give the <u>highest product</u>.

E.g. Partition the number into a large number of small numbers, but don't use the number 1. For example, for 12, the highest product possible with 4 numbers (3 × 3 × 3 × 3 = 81) was higher than the highest possible with 2 or 3 numbers.

Section Two — Multiplication and Division

The numbers are now getting a bit larger so children will need to multiply 2-digit numbers by 1-digit numbers, e.g. 3 × 3 × 3 × 3 = 9 × 3 × 3 = 27 × 3 = 81. They could use partitioning for this, or short multiplication.

• Ask each member of the class for their highest product to check this.

• Children should realise that, in order to get the maximum product, they want to avoid multiplying very small numbers together, but they also want to be multiplying lots of numbers together — there's a trade-off.

Extra Support

If children are struggling, show them 3 × 3 × 3 × 3 = 81 and 3 × 3 × 4 × 2 = 72. Ask them what this shows about the numbers needed to make the highest product. The additional 3 × 3 creates a greater product (9) than the extra 4 × 2 (8) despite 4 being a bigger number than 3.

• The complete rule would state that the number 1 should be avoided and there should be as many 3s as possible. However, children may not have worked this out yet — they will have the opportunity to test and refine their rule on the next page.

• The reasoning behind smaller numbers (but not 1) being better is that, for numbers greater than 4, the product of the partitioned numbers is greater than the sum. E.g. if one of the numbers in the partition is 5, then the other numbers would be multiplied by 5 when finding the product. But, if that 5 had been partitioned into 2 and 3, then the other numbers would be multiplied by 6 (because 2 × 3 = 6), so the final product would be higher.

Extra Challenge

An extension to this task could involve pupils being asked what the lowest number was, or if a lower number could be made with more or fewer numbers.

Partitions and Products

22

(7) Using your rule, <u>predict</u> which way of partitioning <u>18</u> will give you the highest product.

Children will need calculators to carry out some of the multiplications.

 I predict that the best way to partition 18 is:

2 + 2 + 2 + 2 + 2 + 2 + 2 + 2 + 2 ....

Now <u>test</u> your prediction by finding the product of your partition, then seeing if you can find a way to get a higher product.

$2 \times 2 \times 2 \times 2 \times 2 \times 2 \times 2 \times 2 \times 2 = 512$

$4 \times 4 \times 4 \times 3 \times 3 = 576$

$2 \times 2 \times 2 \times 2 \times 2 \times 4 \times 4 = 512$

$2 \times 2 \times 2 \times 2 \times 2 \times 2 \times 3 \times 3 = 576$

$2 \times 2 \times 2 \times 3 \times 3 \times 3 \times 3 = 648$

$3 \times 3 \times 3 \times 3 \times 3 \times 3 = 729$

The highest product I could find was ...729..., which I made by multiplying these numbers: $3 \times 3 \times 3 \times 3 \times 3 \times 3$.

Note that when you partition the number 4 into 2 + 2, the product and the sum are the same: $2 + 2 = 2 \times 2 = 4$. So it doesn't make a difference whether pupils use two 2s or one 4.

Pupils may notice that 3s seem to be better than 2s. E.g. if you partition 6, it's better as 3 + 3 (giving a product of 9) than 2 + 2 + 2 (giving a product of 8). If they haven't noticed this, they could be prompted using the challenge below.

Show your thinking

Did your rule work? Is there a way you could change your rule to make it better?

 E.g. My rule wasn't quite right, because using 3s instead of 2s seems to work better. I would change my rule to say that you should partition the number into as many 3s as possible.

Ask children the following: Which is better to partition your number into when trying to produce a higher product: 2s or 3s? Try this out with the numbers 6, 8 and 9. Answer: for these numbers, they will always get a higher product if they use the maximum number of 3s.

 Sharky Sawnose says: "For the partitions of some <u>numbers below 10</u>, you can't produce a product greater than the original number." Explain whether or not Sharky Sawnose is correct.

Now Try This

Section Two — Multiplication and Division

Sharky Sawnose is correct. E.g. When 4 is partitioned into 2 + 2, the product of 2×2 is 4, which is the same as the original number. All other possible partitions produce products that are less than 4: $4 = 3 + 1$: $3 \times 1 = 3$. $4 = 1 + 1 + 1 + 1$: $1 \times 1 \times 1 \times 1 = 1$. $4 = 1 + 1 + 2$: $1 \times 1 \times 2 = 2$.

Children could also go on to find out how many numbers below 10 can't be partitioned to produce a product greater than the original number.

Showing Greater Depth

Children working at Greater Depth will:

- demonstrate that they understand why it is better to partition numbers down to 3s (and 2s if necessary).

- be able to refine their rule in Q7 so it's a set of instructions to find the partition with the highest product: Divide the number by 3 to give the number of 3s. If the remainder is 2, just use that 2. If the remainder is 1, subtract another 3 and turn that into two 2s (or a 4). E.g.
  20: $20 \div 3 = 6$ r2. So the highest product will be: $3 \times 3 \times 3 \times 3 \times 3 \times 3 \times 2 = 1458$.
  19: $19 \div 3 = 6$ r1. So the highest product will be: $3 \times 3 \times 3 \times 3 \times 3 \times 2 \times 2 = 972$.

Comparing Fractions

Children need to understand the link between fractions and division. They'll be creating their own fraction wall with strips of paper placed horizontally underneath one another. Each strip of paper will be presented as a number line. From their fraction wall, they'll generate a range of equivalent fractions.

Aims:

- Recognise and show equivalent fractions in a visual way.

- Understand the link between division and fractions.

- Understand that being methodical helps to find every answer possible.

Key Vocabulary:

'equivalent fractions', 'halves', 'thirds', 'quarters', 'fifths', 'sixths', 'eighths', 'twelfths'

Resources Needed:

Strips of plain coloured paper, ruler, glue, scissors.

Printable coloured strips available at:

cgpbooks.co.uk/KS2-Maths-Investigations

Year 4 Pupil Book — page 23

Section Three — Fractions   23

Comparing Fractions

Warm Up Questions

1) Colour in the given fraction of each shape below.

E.g. a) $\frac{6}{8}$ b) $\frac{1}{3}$ c) $\frac{1}{4}$

2) What fraction of each of these shapes is coloured in?

a) $\frac{2}{3}$ b) $\frac{3}{4}$ c) $\frac{3}{5}$

3) Put circles around the shapes from Questions 1 and 2 that show equivalent fractions.

① You are going to make your own <u>fraction wall</u>, using strips of different coloured paper that are 12 cm long.

Take the first strip of paper and mark 0 at the start, 1 at the end, and mark it at half way with $\frac{1}{2}$.

Take your time here, to make sure your fraction wall is accurate.

How many centimetres along the strip did you mark $\frac{1}{2}$?

6 cm

Glue the strip onto the top section of the grid on the next page.

Section Three — Fractions

Extra Support

If children struggle with 3), ask them how many parts they would colour for $\frac{1}{4}$ on a shape divided into eighths. Discuss the relationship between $\frac{1}{4}$ and $\frac{1}{8}$ and then ask them how they could work out how many parts to colour for $\frac{3}{4}$.

Children can make these strips themselves, or they can have the printed versions available online.

Comparing Fractions

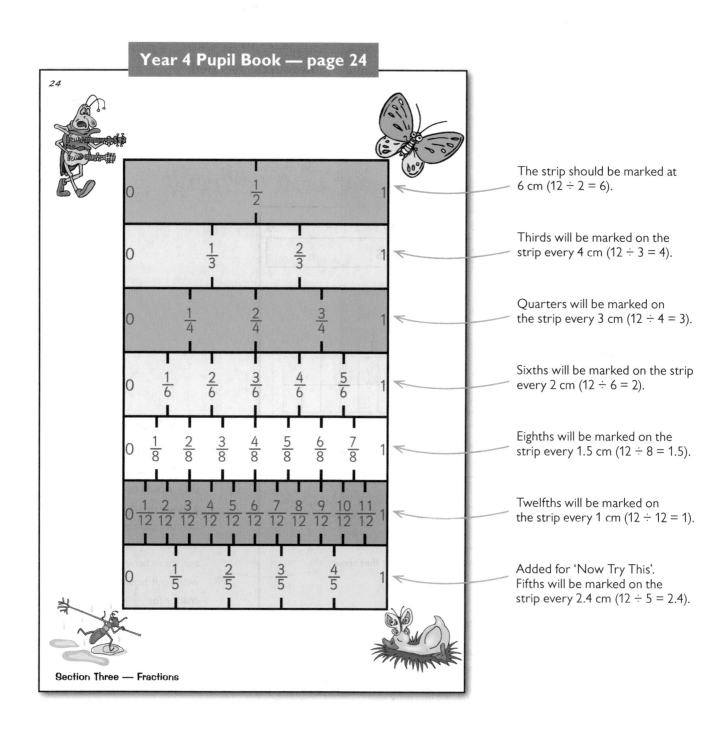

24

$0 \quad \frac{1}{2} \quad 1$

$0 \quad \frac{1}{3} \quad \frac{2}{3} \quad 1$

$0 \quad \frac{1}{4} \quad \frac{2}{4} \quad \frac{3}{4} \quad 1$

$0 \quad \frac{1}{6} \quad \frac{2}{6} \quad \frac{3}{6} \quad \frac{4}{6} \quad \frac{5}{6} \quad 1$

$0 \quad \frac{1}{8} \quad \frac{2}{8} \quad \frac{3}{8} \quad \frac{4}{8} \quad \frac{5}{8} \quad \frac{6}{8} \quad \frac{7}{8} \quad 1$

$0 \quad \frac{1}{12} \quad \frac{2}{12} \quad \frac{3}{12} \quad \frac{4}{12} \quad \frac{5}{12} \quad \frac{6}{12} \quad \frac{7}{12} \quad \frac{8}{12} \quad \frac{9}{12} \quad \frac{10}{12} \quad \frac{11}{12} \quad 1$

$0 \quad \frac{1}{5} \quad \frac{2}{5} \quad \frac{3}{5} \quad \frac{4}{5} \quad 1$

The strip should be marked at 6 cm (12 ÷ 2 = 6).

Thirds will be marked on the strip every 4 cm (12 ÷ 3 = 4).

Quarters will be marked on the strip every 3 cm (12 ÷ 4 = 3).

Sixths will be marked on the strip every 2 cm (12 ÷ 6 = 2).

Eighths will be marked on the strip every 1.5 cm (12 ÷ 8 = 1.5).

Twelfths will be marked on the strip every 1 cm (12 ÷ 12 = 1).

Added for 'Now Try This'. Fifths will be marked on the strip every 2.4 cm (12 ÷ 5 = 2.4).

Section Three — Fractions

Comparing Fractions

25

(2) With your second strip of paper, mark 0 at the start and 1 at the end. Then mark $\frac{1}{3}$ and $\frac{2}{3}$ at the correct places.

$\frac{1}{3}$ should be at 4 cm. Where is $\frac{2}{3}$?

_8_ cm

Glue the strip onto the thirds section of the grid.

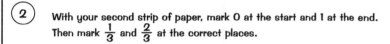

(3) With your third strip of paper, mark 0 and 1. Then mark $\frac{1}{4}$, $\frac{2}{4}$ and $\frac{3}{4}$ at the correct places. Complete the sentence below.

I marked $\frac{1}{4}$ at _3_ cm, $\frac{2}{4}$ at _6_ cm and $\frac{3}{4}$ at _9_ cm.

Glue the strip onto the quarters section of the grid.

You should be getting the hang of this by now.

(4) Continue marking up strips of paper and gluing them onto the grid to show <u>sixths</u>, <u>eighths</u> and <u>twelfths</u>. Then complete the sentences below.

I marked sixths every _2_ cm along the strip.

I marked eighths every _1.5_ cm along the strip.

I marked twelfths every _1_ cm along the strip.

Eighths are a bit tricky -- the number of centimetres between each mark will not be a whole number.

Section Three — Fractions

Extra Support

Pupils who are struggling should be encouraged to begin by answering $\frac{1}{4}$, then scaling up.

Extra Challenge

Ask more able children why eighths are marked at 1.5 cm. They may be able to explain that $1.5 = 1\frac{1}{2}$, and 12 divided by 8 is $1\frac{1}{2}$, i.e. 1 lot of 8 and half of 8 (4) makes 12.
This idea could also be discussed in pairs.

Comparing Fractions

26

⑤ Look at your fraction wall. Find a fraction on one row that has been marked in the same position as a fraction on another row. These are <u>equivalent fractions</u>. Find sets of equivalent fractions and write them out below.

E.g. $\frac{1}{3} = \frac{2}{6} = \frac{4}{12}$

Try to find some sets that contain more than just two equivalent fractions.

$\frac{1}{2} = \frac{2}{4} = \frac{3}{6} = \frac{4}{8} = \frac{6}{12}$

$\frac{1}{3} = \frac{2}{6} = \frac{4}{12}$

$\frac{2}{3} = \frac{4}{6} = \frac{8}{12}$

$\frac{1}{4} = \frac{2}{8} = \frac{3}{12}$ $\frac{1}{6} = \frac{2}{12}$

$\frac{3}{4} = \frac{6}{8} = \frac{9}{12}$ $\frac{5}{6} = \frac{10}{12}$

• For those who are able, encourage children to find ALL equivalent fractions for each set rather than a pair of equivalent fractions.

• Those who are struggling could be encouraged to focus on the unit fractions, e.g. $\frac{1}{2}$, $\frac{1}{3}$.

Show your thinking

Write down how you have been <u>methodical</u>.

E.g. I did all the unit fractions first, then those with 2 as the numerator, 3 as the numerator, and so on. / I worked through the fraction wall from top to bottom (halves then thirds then quarters etc.).

• Some pupils may need to be told that this will be at 2.4 cm intervals.

• Others may be able to work it out, either with the use of a calculator, or using a written division method (this may lead them to find that $12 \div 5 = 2\frac{2}{5}$ — in Year 4, they are not yet expected to know the decimal equivalent of $\frac{2}{5}$ so are likely to need help.

You will need to add a fifths strip to your wall. Where will you mark each fifth?

Now Try This With a partner, take it in turns to throw two dice each. Use the smaller number you throw as the numerator, and the larger as the denominator. If the two numbers are the same, then the fraction is 1. Use your fraction wall to help work out whose fraction is bigger. This person wins a point. Play until one of you has 10 points.

Answers will vary, e.g. $\frac{1}{3} < \frac{5}{6}$, $\frac{3}{4} > \frac{2}{3}$, $\frac{3}{5} > \frac{2}{4}$

Section Three — Fractions   😟 ☑   🙂 ☑   😃 ☑

Showing Greater Depth

Children working at Greater Depth will:

• (Q5) be systematic in their thinking in order to come up with all the possible sets of equivalent fractions. They should also be able to describe <u>how</u> they have worked methodically.

Number Rod Fractions

Children need to be able to recognise fractions from visual representations. They'll be creating their own visual fractions using number rods (if these are not available, paper copies can be printed). They'll be using visual representations to help add fractions with the same denominator. They'll generate a range of calculations, think about how to work systematically and recognise that fractions can be greater than 1.

Aims:

- Show fractions in a visual way.

- Add and subtract fractions with the same denominator.

- Recognise that fractions go beyond 1 whole.

Key Vocabulary:

'numerator', 'denominator'

Resources Needed:

Number rods.
Printable number rods available at:

cgpbooks.co.uk/KS2-Maths-Investigations

Year 4 Pupil Book — page 27

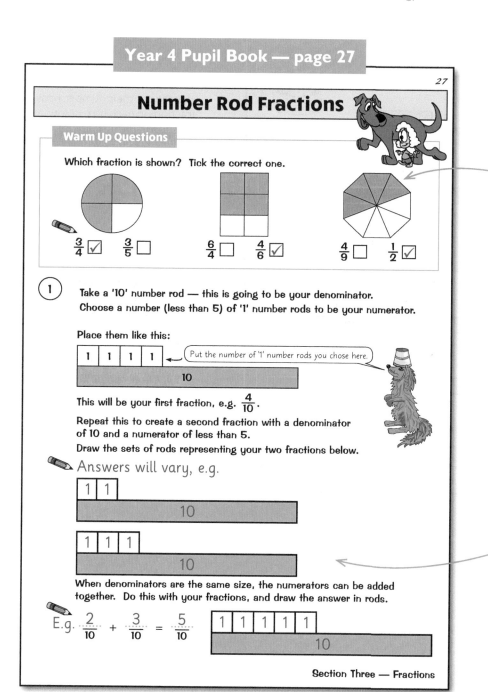

- The choices in the second question are there to make sure children know the difference between the numerator and the denominator.

- The choices in the third question are there to make sure children know it is not just the numerator that is key to a fraction. Even though 4 pieces are shaded, there are not 9 pieces in total. This fraction is $\frac{1}{2}$ of the overall shape.

- At this stage, children should be adding the numerators (less than 5) so that they create a total numerator less than 10.

- Whilst the pictures children draw of the rods do not have to be accurate in length, it is useful to colour them the same as the actual rods and/or label them with the correct numbers.

Number Rod Fractions

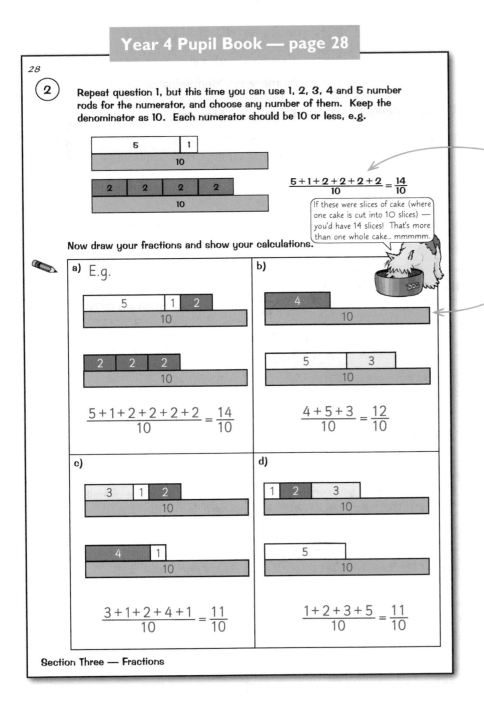

28

(2) Repeat question 1, but this time you can use 1, 2, 3, 4 and 5 number rods for the numerator, and choose any number of them. Keep the denominator as 10. Each numerator should be 10 or less, e.g.

| 5 | 1 |

| 10 |

| 2 | 2 | 2 | 2 |

| 10 |

$$\frac{5+1+2+2+2+2}{10} = \frac{14}{10}$$

If these were slices of cake (where one cake is cut into 10 slices) — you'd have 14 slices! That's more than one whole cake... mmmmm.

Now draw your fractions and show your calculations.

a) E.g.

| 5 | 1 | 2 |

| 10 |

| 2 | 2 | 2 |

| 10 |

$$\frac{5+1+2+2+2+2}{10} = \frac{14}{10}$$

b)

| 4 |

| 10 |

| 5 | 3 |

| 10 |

$$\frac{4+5+3}{10} = \frac{12}{10}$$

c)

| 3 | 1 | 2 |

| 10 |

| 4 | 1 |

| 10 |

$$\frac{3+1+2+4+1}{10} = \frac{11}{10}$$

d)

| 1 | 2 | 3 |

| 10 |

| 5 |

| 10 |

$$\frac{1+2+3+5}{10} = \frac{11}{10}$$

Section Three — Fractions

This question reinforces the fact that, where denominators are the same in a calculation, the denominator in the answer will be the same. A common mistake is for pupils to add two fractions with a denominator of 10, and change the denominator to 20.

Children should make simple sketches of their number rods as fractions in each box, colour and/ or label them and show the calculation generated.

Extra Challenge

Ask more able children to also write each fraction they've created with their rods as a fraction with a single numerator. Then they can add them together, and should get the same answer. E.g. for a) they would write:

$$\frac{8}{10} + \frac{6}{10} = \frac{14}{10}.$$

Number Rod Fractions

29

(3) Use number rods to show the following fractions:

$$\frac{3}{5} \quad \frac{5}{10} \quad \frac{7}{10} \quad \frac{1}{5} \quad \frac{2}{3} \quad \frac{4}{3} \quad \frac{4}{5}$$

Use the fractions to generate different fraction additions. How many can you find?

Remember, you can only add numerators if the denominators are the same size.

It won't always be '10' rods on the denominator this time.

$$\frac{2}{3} + \frac{4}{3} = \frac{6}{3}$$

$$\frac{5}{10} + \frac{7}{10} = \frac{12}{10}$$

$$\frac{3}{5} + \frac{1}{5} = \frac{4}{5} \qquad \frac{1}{5} + \frac{4}{5} = \frac{5}{5} = 1 \qquad \frac{3}{5} + \frac{4}{5} = \frac{7}{5}$$

$$\frac{3}{5} + \frac{1}{5} + \frac{4}{5} = \frac{8}{5}$$

I found ....6.... different additions.

Children should have found a minimum of 4 additions (possibly not finding all 3 combinations of adding fifths). When they understand more than 2 fractions can be added together, a sixth addition is possible.

Show your thinking

Have you found all of the possible additions? If yes, how do you know? If not, how could you find more?

E.g. I have found them all. I know this because there are just two fractions with 3 as the denominator, so there's only one way of adding those. The same is true for the tenths. With the fifths, there are 3 possible pairs that can be added, and then the final addition was all three of them together.

Just like you can add up 3 numbers (e.g. 7 + 5 + 4), you can add up 3 fractions. Does this change the number of different additions you can find?

• There are different variations of how the numerators can be shown, e.g.:

2	2	1	2	3	2
5					

Now Try This

Show the fraction $\frac{12}{5}$ using number rods. By subtracting different combinations of number rods from the numerator, what different subtraction calculations can you generate?

Section Three — Fractions

• Answers will vary, but will range from $\frac{12}{5} - \frac{1}{5} = \frac{11}{5}$ to $\frac{12}{5} - \frac{11}{5} = \frac{1}{5}$.

It will help to physically remove the number rods that make the fraction they subtract from the numerator. They could then shift the numerator rods up to see how many are left in total.

Showing Greater Depth

Children working at Greater Depth will:

• (Q3) think about how to generate all the possible different additions, including showing organisation in their work by grouping their additions — thirds, fifths and tenths.

Rectangles

In this investigation, children will find the perimeters of rectangles given their dimensions. They will also find areas of rectangles by counting squares, and consider the relationship between a rectangle's dimensions and its area. Children should be familiar with the 2, 3 and 4 times tables.

Aims:

- Calculate the perimeters of rectangles in cm.

- Calculate the areas of rectangles by counting squares.

- Notice connections between dimensions, area and perimeter.

Key Vocabulary:

'area', 'perimeter', 'length', 'width'

Resources Needed:

1 cm squared paper, scissors, glue, colouring pencils. Centimetre cubes may be useful for some children. Printable squared paper available at:

cgpbooks.co.uk/KS2-Maths-Investigations

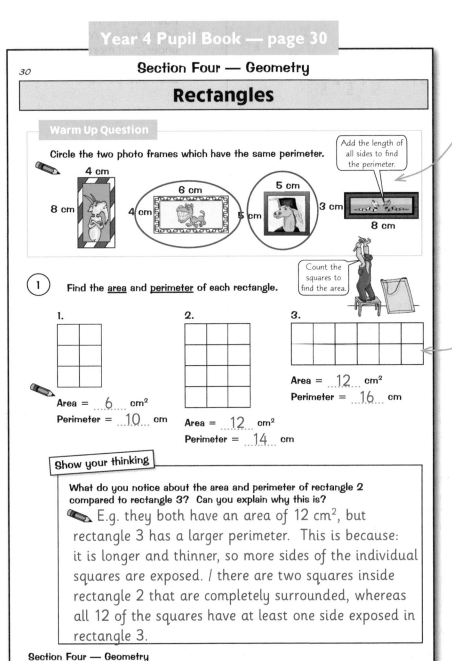

- The perimeter of a shape is the distance around its edge.

- From left to right, these perimeters are: 24 cm, 20 cm, 20 cm and 22 cm.

- Some children may recognise that the perimeter can be found by doubling the length, doubling the width and adding together. In the case of a square, they may notice that you can multiply the side length by 4.

- To avoid errors when finding the area, encourage children to place a dot in each square they count.

- To avoid errors when finding the perimeter, a little dash can be marked across each square side counted.

- Reinforce to pupils that the unit for area must end with the 'squared' symbol (^{2}) as there are two dimensions for 2D shapes — length and width.

Rectangles

- Encourage children to think of factor pairs that can make up 24.

- The following rectangles should be drawn:
  3 cm × 8 cm,
  6 cm × 4 cm,
  12 cm × 2 cm,
  24 cm × 1 cm.

- Each rectangle's width and length could be the other way round.

Extra Support

If children struggle to find all 4 rectangles, they could try arranging 24 centimetre cubes in rectangles.

Extra Challenge

Some children may be able to explain why the perimeters are all even. It is because they are formed by adding double the length to double the width (or by doubling the sum of the length and the width). Doubles are always even.

31

2 On your squared paper, draw <u>four different rectangles</u>, each with an area of **24 cm²**, i.e. they are made up of **24 squares**. Colour each rectangle a different colour.
Write down the <u>length</u> and <u>width</u> of each rectangle in the table below.

Rectangle	A	B	C	D
Length (cm)	24	12	8	6
Width (cm)	1	2	3	4

Show your thinking

How do the length and width of each rectangle relate to its area?

E.g. The area of each rectangle is the length multiplied by its width. For example, in shape A: 24 × 1 = 24, the same as the area. / The length and width are a factor pair of 24, so multiply to give 24 (the area).

3 Find the <u>perimeter</u> of each of your rectangles.

Rectangle	A	B	C	D
Perimeter (cm)	50	28	22	20

What do you notice about the perimeters?

E.g. they are all different/even.

4 Now <u>cut your rectangles out</u> and stick them on the grid on the next page to form a giant shape. Each rectangle must <u>touch</u> at least one other rectangle along a side. Find the <u>perimeter</u> and <u>area</u> of your new shape.

Section Four — Geometry

Children should be encouraged to add the correct units for perimeter and area.

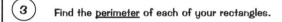

Rectangles

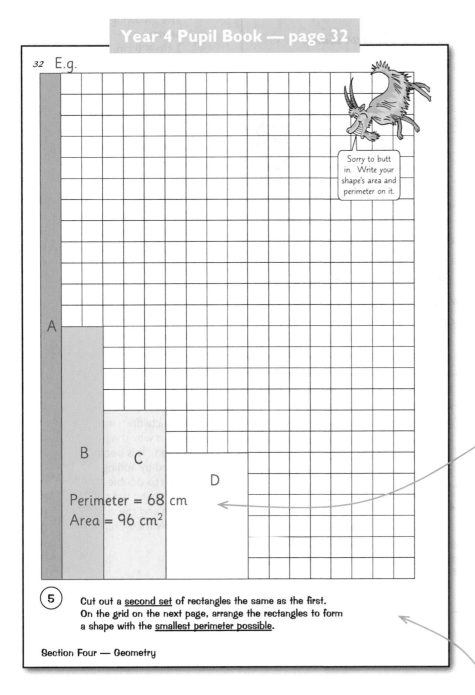

32 E.g.

Sorry to butt in. Write your shape's area and perimeter on it.

A

B   C

D

Perimeter = 68 cm
Area = 96 cm²

5 Cut out a <u>second set</u> of rectangles the same as the first.
On the grid on the next page, arrange the rectangles to form
a shape with the <u>smallest perimeter possible</u>.

Section Four — Geometry

- Make sure the children position their rectangles so that each corner lies on the intersection of two gridlines. This will make calculating the perimeters easier.

- Children might realise that the sum of the horizontal lengths at the top of the shape is equal to the sum of the horizontal lengths at the bottom of the shape. The sums are both 10 cm in the example shown. The same is true of the sums of the vertical lengths on the left and right of the shape (24 cm in this example).

It will be interesting to discuss the areas and perimeters calculated by members of the class.

- The area will always be 96 cm², however the rectangles are placed.

- The perimeter will vary, depending on which of the rectangles' sides are touching.

- Encourage children to discuss strategies for minimising the perimeter with each other.

- The 24 cm × 1 cm rectangle can only go in one orientation, but the other rectangles can be rotated 90 degrees.

Rectangles

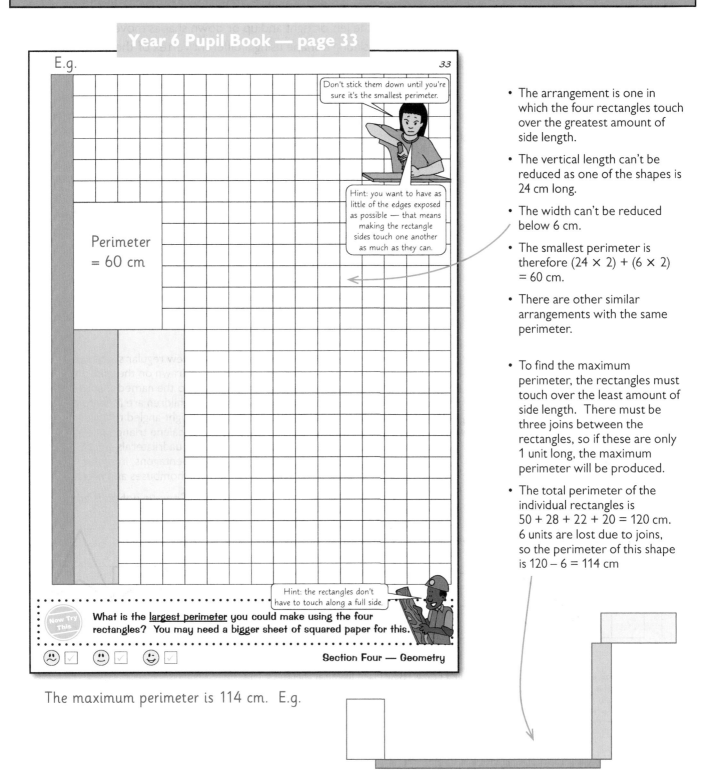

Year 6 Pupil Book — page 33

E.g. *33*

Don't stick them down until you're sure it's the smallest perimeter.

Hint: you want to have as little of the edges exposed as possible — that means making the rectangle sides touch one another as much as they can.

Perimeter = 60 cm

- The arrangement is one in which the four rectangles touch over the greatest amount of side length.
- The vertical length can't be reduced as one of the shapes is 24 cm long.
- The width can't be reduced below 6 cm.
- The smallest perimeter is therefore (24 × 2) + (6 × 2) = 60 cm.
- There are other similar arrangements with the same perimeter.

- To find the maximum perimeter, the rectangles must touch over the least amount of side length. There must be three joins between the rectangles, so if these are only 1 unit long, the maximum perimeter will be produced.
- The total perimeter of the individual rectangles is 50 + 28 + 22 + 20 = 120 cm. 6 units are lost due to joins, so the perimeter of this shape is 120 − 6 = 114 cm

Hint: the rectangles don't have to touch along a full side.

Now Try This What is the largest perimeter you could make using the four rectangles? You may need a bigger sheet of squared paper for this.

Section Four — Geometry

The maximum perimeter is 114 cm. E.g.

Showing Greater Depth

Children working at Greater Depth will:

- (Q1) explain how two rectangles can have the same area but different perimeters.
- (Q2) identify and describe the relationship between the dimensions and area of a rectangle.
- (Q5 and Now Try This) explain how they know they have found the shape with the smallest or largest perimeter.

Triangle Translations

In this investigation, children count how many units to the left or right and up or down shapes move to reach a new position. They'll also investigate the effect of translating a shape using a different vertex of the shape, and generate a rule for reversing a translation.

Aims:

- Classify shapes using geometrical properties.
- Describe movements between positions as translations of a given unit to the left/right and up/down.
- Generate a rule by noticing patterns.

Key Vocabulary:

'vertex', 'translate', 'orientation'

Resources Needed:

Colouring pencils,
1 cm squared paper,
small pieces of card, scissors.
Printable squared paper available at:
cgpbooks.co.uk/KS2-Maths-Investigations

Year 4 Pupil Book — page 34

34

Triangle Translations

Warm Up Questions

Draw 4 more <u>different shapes</u> on the grid below and colour them in.
Label each shape with a number and write its name.
One has been done for you.

E.g.

1. isosceles triangle
2. kite
3. trapezium
4. square
5. parallelogram

- Few regular shapes can be drawn on the grid. In addition to the named shapes shown, children are likely to draw right-angled triangles and scalene triangles, irregular quadrilaterals, irregular pentagons, irregular hexagons, rhombuses and rectangles.

- Concave polygons are also possible. E.g.

Concave   Inverted
pentagon   kite

(1) Look at the shape S drawn on the grid below. How many identical shapes in the <u>same orientation</u> can you find on the grid?
Draw them on the grid and give each a new number. One is done for you.

E.g.

> Watch out! 'Same orientation' means 'same way up', so make sure you don't flip the shape over, or turn it around.

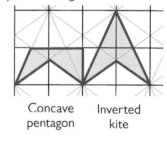

- There are four more identical shapes children could have found. They occur on the same rows as the two shapes already shown, within alternating squares.

- The numbering will vary depending on the order in which the shapes are found.

Section Four — Geometry

Triangle Translations

35

(2) The starting shape S has been <u>translated</u> (or moved) to shape 1.

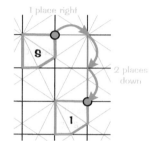

Choose the same <u>vertex</u> (corner) on both shapes and mark it with a dot.

Then see how far the dot on shape S must slide <u>across</u> and <u>down</u> to get to the position of the dot on shape 1.

It moves <u>1 place right and 2 places down</u>. This is the <u>translation</u>.

The shape can only move along the black horizontal and vertical lines, so choose a <u>vertex</u> that lies on them.

The heavy black grid is what the shape is being translated around. The grey lines were just to help children draw shapes.

Work out the translations to move shape S to the positions of the other shapes you found in question 1. Record the translations below.

E.g. Shape S → Shape 1 = 1 place right, 2 places down

Shape S → Shape 2 = ...2 places right.........................

Shape S → Shape 3 = ...4 places right.........................

Shape S → Shape 4 = ...3 places right, 2 places down......

Shape S → Shape 5 = ...1 place left, 2 places down........

- Children may give the up/down part of the translation before the left/right part. Although this is fine at this stage, in standard translations, the horizontal movement is given before the vertical, so modelling the translations this way is useful.

- Children might also give the translation in more than two steps. E.g. Shape S to Shape 4 can also be give as 4 places right, 2 places down, 1 place left.

- These will be in a different order if children have numbered their shapes differently.

(3) Try some of the translations again, but this time use a <u>different vertex</u>. <u>Compare</u> the new translations to the ones found using the original vertex. What do you notice?

....The translations are the same whichever vertex....

....you use...

Children may choose any vertex to translate from. However the vertices at the bottom-right of the shape don't sit on both horizontal and vertical grid lines, so are best avoided.

Section Four — Geometry

Extra Challenge

Ask children to write down the translations between other shapes, e.g. Shapes 3 and 4.

Triangle Translations

36

(4) Draw one <u>different shape</u> on the grid at least <u>4 times</u>.
Label your first shape S and the other shapes 1, 2 and 3.
Work out the <u>translations</u> from one shape to another
and record them below.

E.g.

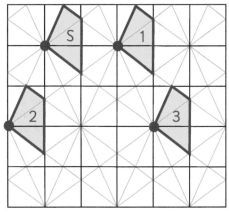

Remember to
show the vertex
you are translating
with a big dot.

Shape S → Shape 1 = 2 places right

Shape S → Shape 2 = 1 place left, 2 places down

Shape S → Shape 3 = 3 places right, 2 places down

Write at least 2 more translations between the shapes you've drawn.

Shape 1 → Shape 2

= 3 places left, 2 places down

Shape 3 → Shape 2

= 4 places left

Section Four — Geometry

- If children have chosen a shape that uses the black grid lines, such as a square or rectangle, encourage them to draw the shapes dotted around the grid, not in a straight line.

- Encourage children to choose a suitable vertex, i.e. one that lies on the intersection of the black grid lines.

Answers will vary, so children could check each other's translations.

Triangle Translations

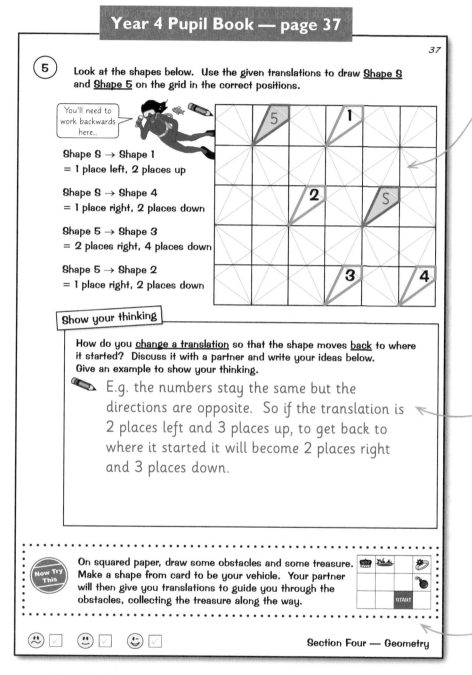

Two of the translations given involve shape S, and two involve shape 5. Encourage children to use the second translation for each to check their positioning is correct.

- Children will need to compare the translations between 2 shapes, e.g.
Shape 5 → Shape 2:
1 place right, 2 places down
Shape 2 → Shape 5:
1 place left, 2 places up

- To check that what they notice is a rule, they should compare the translations between at least one more pair of shapes.

- It may need to be reinforced that this activity must be solvable, and not just obstacle after obstacle that make it impossible to solve.

- It's important that children don't turn their 'vehicle'. It must slide left/right and up/down on the grid.

E.g. 2 places up, 1 place right, 1 place left, 1 place down...

Showing Greater Depth

Children working at Greater Depth will:

- (Q5) select appropriate pairs of translations and analyse them to generate a rule for reversing a translation. They will test the rule on other pairs of translations and justify why it will always work.

Symmetry

Children need to be familiar with common 2D shapes and their names. They'll be identifying and drawing lines of symmetry in given shapes. They'll be comparing shapes with the same number of sides but a different number of lines of symmetry, and looking for a pattern. By counting from points to the line of symmetry, children will complete the drawing of symmetrical shapes.

Aims:

- Identify lines of symmetry in 2D shapes.

- Complete a symmetrical figure with respect to a specific line of symmetry.

- Classify shapes according to the number of lines of symmetry they have.

Key Vocabulary:

'regular', 'irregular', 'horizontal', 'vertical', 'diagonal'

Resources Needed:

Squared paper, mirror, ruler.
Printable squared paper available at:

cgpbooks.co.uk/KS2-Maths-Investigations

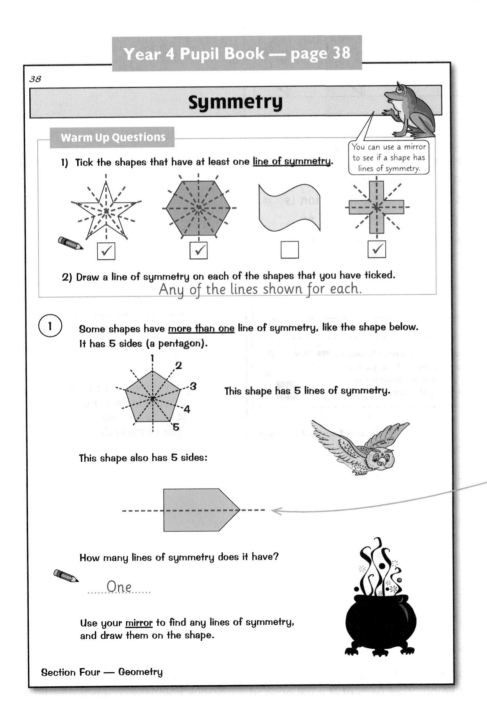

Some children may see where the line of symmetry is immediately while others may need to use the mirror (vertically, horizontally and diagonally) to find it.

Symmetry

Year 4 Pupil Book — page 39

39

Show your thinking

Why do you think the first pentagon had 5 lines of symmetry but the second pentagon didn't?

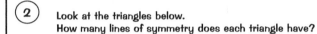 The first pentagon is regular (or all of its sides are the same length). In the second pentagon, the horizontal sides are the same length as each other and the diagonal sides are the same length as each other, so there's only one line of symmetry.

Pupils may notice the first pentagon is regular, but might not use this term to describe it — try to encourage the use of the terms 'regular' and 'irregular' wherever possible.

(2) Look at the triangles below.
How many lines of symmetry does each triangle have?

Sometimes rotating (turning) the shape makes it easier to spot lines of symmetry. Try rotating the book to help you.

This triangle has ___3___ line(s) of symmetry.

This triangle has ___1___ line(s) of symmetry.

- Children should notice that the first triangle has three equal sides, and the second triangle has two equal sides. Discussion with their partners might help with this.

- If children struggle, ask them to compare the number of lines of symmetry with the number of equal sides.

Show your thinking

What do you notice about the symmetry of these shapes? Why do you think this is?

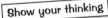 Even though they are both triangles, the first has more lines of symmetry than the second. This is because the first triangle is regular (equilateral), so a line can be drawn from each corner to the middle of the opposite side, but the second is isosceles so only has two equal sides.

- In triangle 1, pupils could be encouraged to use their mirror if needed, and to draw the lines on the shape — this will help to avoid forgetting how many lines of symmetry they have already found.

- In triangle 2, it is easier to see where the line of symmetry should go by rotating it so the longest side is horizontal (and then the equal sides are either side of the vertical line of symmetry).

- Encourage pupils to use proper triangle names here.

Section Four — Geometry

Symmetry

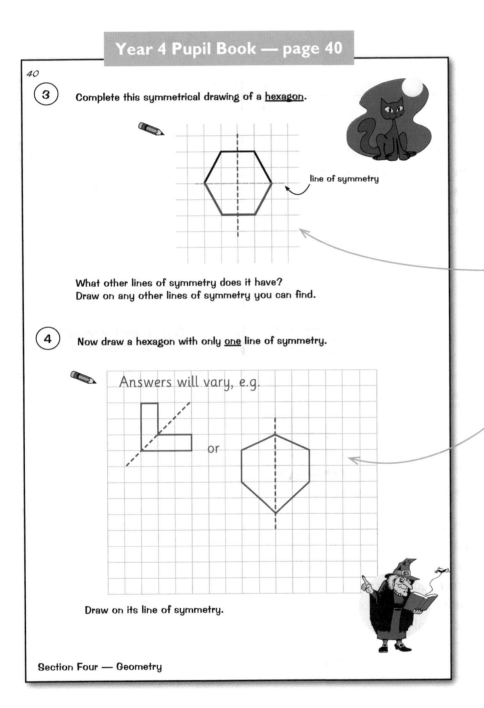

40

3 Complete this symmetrical drawing of a **hexagon**.

line of symmetry

What other lines of symmetry does it have?
Draw on any other lines of symmetry you can find.

4 Now draw a hexagon with only **one** line of symmetry.

Answers will vary, e.g.

or

Draw on its line of symmetry.

Section Four — Geometry

Encourage children to complete the symmetrical hexagon by counting how many squares away from the line of symmetry each point of the shape is.

Extra Support

• For those who struggle to draw a hexagon with just one line of symmetry, it can help to draw the line first and then draw 3 symmetrical lines either side of the line of symmetry.

• Pupils could also be reminded of the regular and irregular triangles from question 2, to help with this question.

Symmetry

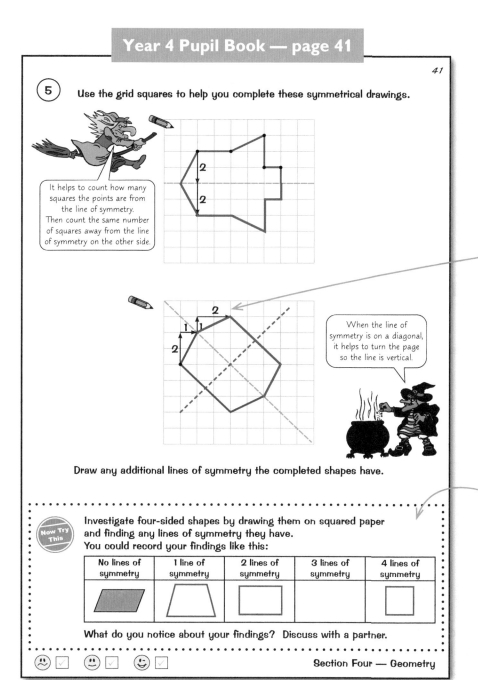

- The arrows show that going up 2 squares and right 1 square becomes up 1 square and right 2 squares on the other side of the line of symmetry.

- Remind children to turn the second picture so that the line of symmetry is vertical.

- It can help to draw spots at the points where lines meet and then count how many squares away from the line of symmetry they are.

Answers will vary and could be written or drawn, e.g.

No lines of symmetry — parallelogram, (irregular) trapezium

1 line of symmetry — kite, (isosceles) trapezium

2 lines of symmetry — rectangle, rhombus

3 lines of symmetry — none

4 lines of symmetry — square

Showing Greater Depth

Children working at Greater Depth will:

- (Q1) compare the two pentagons and consider why they have different numbers of lines of symmetry.
- (Q2) again, analyse the two shapes and consider why, even though they are both triangles, their lines of symmetry are different.

Bar Charts

Children will be reading information from a bar chart to work out where the labels go and how to label the axes correctly. They'll be answering questions based on the information presented. They'll collect data of their own using their choice of recording method, and then use this data to create a bar chart of their own, accurately labelled.

Aims:

- Interpret and present data using bar charts.

- Collect and record data clearly.

- Use a systematic method to collect data (tally marks, ticks etc.).

Key Vocabulary:

'bar chart', 'axes'

Resources Needed:

Ruler. If needed, spare squared paper is available at:

cgpbooks.co.uk/KS2-Maths-Investigations

Year 4 Pupil Book — page 42

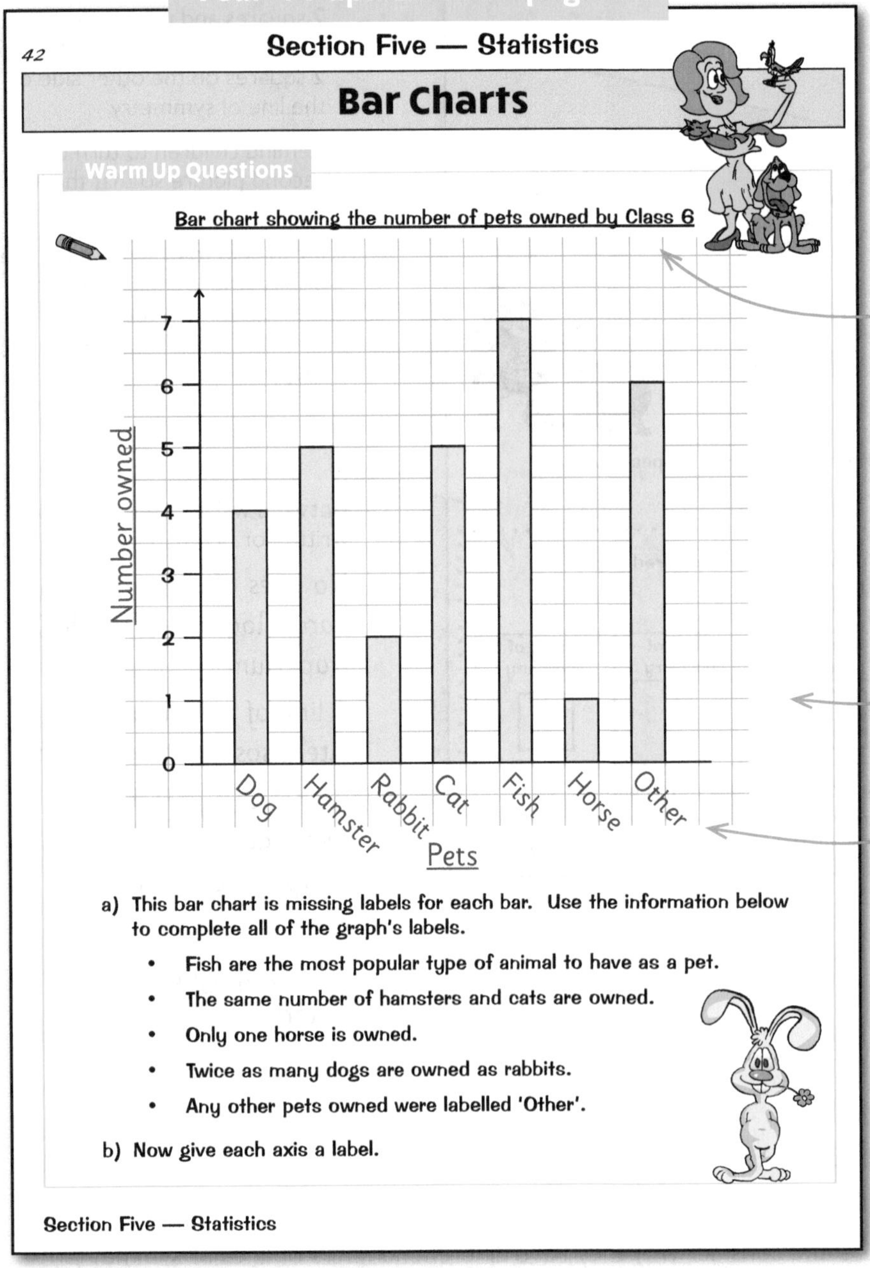

42   **Section Five — Statistics**

Bar Charts

Warm Up Questions

Bar chart showing the number of pets owned by Class 6

[Bar chart: y-axis labelled "Number owned" with values 0 to 7; x-axis labelled "Pets" with categories Dog, Hamster, Rabbit, Cat, Fish, Horse, Other. Bar values: Dog = 4, Hamster = 5, Rabbit = 2, Cat = 5, Fish = 7, Horse = 1, Other = 6]

a) This bar chart is missing labels for each bar. Use the information below to complete all of the graph's labels.
  - Fish are the most popular type of animal to have as a pet.
  - The same number of hamsters and cats are owned.
  - Only one horse is owned.
  - Twice as many dogs are owned as rabbits.
  - Any other pets owned were labelled 'Other'.

b) Now give each axis a label.

Section Five — Statistics

Extra Support

Pupils who are struggling can be encouraged to read the bar chart's title, to get the information they need about what the axes show.

The cat and hamster bars can be labelled in either order.

Warn pupils that they need to label each bar carefully, otherwise they could run out of space or overlap.

Bar Charts

43

1 You are going to investigate how Class 6's pet ownership compares to your school.

Show your thinking

Talk to your partner about the steps you will take to be able to make this comparison. Write your ideas here.

Think about how you will collect and record the data, and then how you will present your data.

Answers should include:

- Ask a number of children what pets they own.
- Record the data using some kind of chart or table.
- Use the information collected to create a bar chart.

- Pupils could ask their whole class, or ask children in the playground at playtime.

- An advantage of asking children in the playground is that each child will get different data, and they'll enjoy the process of selecting who they ask. (Also, the noise level in class when asking will be moved to the playground!)

- Alternatively, pupils could talk to each other on their table and record those answers, and then one pupil can be nominated to move around the other tables to record more results for their table.

2 Collect your data from a group of about 20-30 children and record it with your chosen method.

Answers will vary but should show the different pets with ticks, marks or a tally, e.g.

Dog											
Hamster					
Cat							
Fish									
Tortoise			

Asking 20-30 children will give enough data to create a good bar chart with axes of a reasonable length.

This is an opportunity to get pupils thinking about and discussing why tallies are useful — they allow them to quickly record information before transferring it over to a bar chart.

3 Use the axes on the next page to show the data you have collected in a bar chart.

Section Five — Statistics

Bar Charts

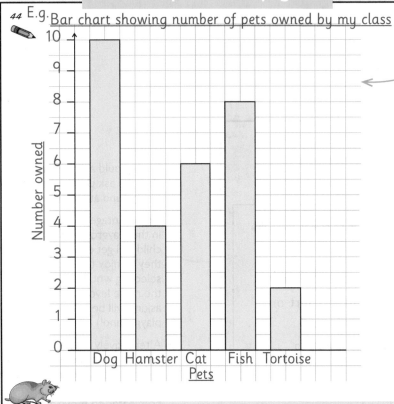

44 E.g. Bar chart showing number of pets owned by my class

(4) Compare your data with that of Class 6. What do you notice?

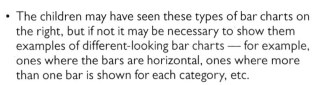

Answers will vary, e.g. my class has more dogs than Class 6. Someone in Class 6 has a horse, but no one in my class does. The pet that my class has the most of is dogs, but in Class 6 it is fish.

Sergeant Statistics says it is possible to show both classes' data about their pets on one bar chart. Discuss with your partner how this could be done and then give it a go.

Section Five — Statistics

- If the pupils' results won't fit neatly onto a bar chart on these axes, they can be given spare squared paper (printable squared paper is available as an online resource).

- A discussion with the class about 'success criteria' for a good bar chart could be held ahead of drawing theirs. Points discussed should include:
  - Using the lines of the squared paper as a guide to draw equal markers.
  - Labelling each axis and give the bar chart a title.
  - Equal width bars with equal gaps between them.

- Putting the pets in the same order along the horizontal axis as they were in the warm-up question will help with the comparison in question 4.

- Depending on the variety of pets in the answers, pupils may need to have an 'Other' category, as was seen in the warm up question, rather than having a bar for every type of pet.

Remind children to write down similarities and differences.

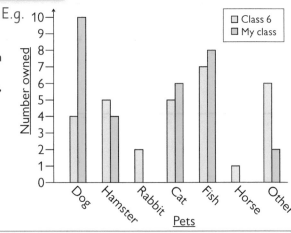

Bar chart showing pet ownership in my class and in Class 6

- The children may have seen these types of bar charts on the right, but if not it may be necessary to show them examples of different-looking bar charts — for example, ones where the bars are horizontal, ones where more than one bar is shown for each category, etc.

- Point out to children that this type of bar chart needs a key to show which bars show which set of data.

Showing Greater Depth

Children working at Greater Depth will:
- (Q1) come up with a sensible system for collecting data, e.g. drawing a tally table before asking people.